NAKED APE

an anthology
of male chauvinism
from the
Guardian

edited by

Andrew Veitch

D0916261

DUCKWORTH

First published in 1981 by
Gerald Duckworth & Co. Ltd.,
The Old Piano Factory,
43 Gloucester Crescent, London N.W.1.

Foreword and editorial arrangement © 1981 by Andrew Veitch

ISBN 0 7156 1614 5

Printed and bound in Great Britain
by Redwood Burn Ltd, Trowbridge, Wiltshire

Contents

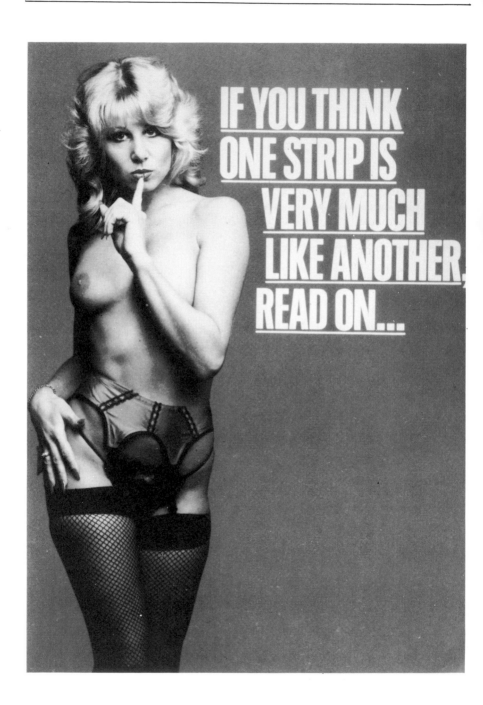

IF YOU THINK ONE STRIP IS VERY MUCH LIKE ANOTHER, READ ON....

Introduction

To Liz Forgan, whose creation this is.

The woman on the cover is being used to sell sticky stuff - a sort of sealing compound. The advertisement in which she appears is one of thousands of examples of the apish art — newspaper reports, advertisements, official letters — submitted by readers.

It all began with Liz Forgan, now a commissioning editor on Channel Four. Upon her desk one morning landed a copy of *Publishing News* in which a certain publisher, asked the secret of his success, replied: 'I price books on the female principle — raise the price as high as possible then lie back and enjoy it.'

It was symptomatic, thought Forgan, and ought to be held up to obloquy. Here is the result.

'Ape is to feminism what brass bands are to the Salvation Army,' she says. 'It is a dose of serious polemic about the cruelty, prejudice, and exploitation of which women are the victims, decked out in jollity to get the message past the reader's instinctive defences.

'First we trap your eye with the typographical bait of the snippet; then we tickle your interest with the promise of a joke; then, snap! the trap is shut and we have got you thinking about unconscious attitudes to women.

'Anyone who thinks that is an example of what are known as "devious feminine wiles" is experiencing unconscious sexism. The recommended cure is to make a list of 300 examples of the use of the phrase, "devious masculine wiles . . ." '

ANDREW VEITCH

AIRTRADE

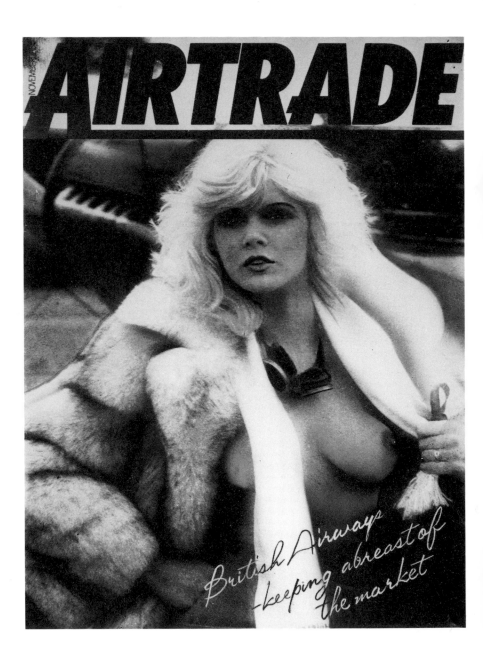

British Airways — keeping abreast of the market

In Judgment

Judge J.W.P. Watts said the only reason he was not sending the man to jail was because the woman was his de facto, and therefore would "not be too upset at being assulted."

Australasian magazine

But the trial judge had not taken fully into account mitigating matters in his favour, said the appeal judge.
The girl at first had allowed him to kiss her and it was only when he became violent that she tried to break away.

Hemel Mail

"A 32-YEAR-OLD Paddock Wood man who beat up his wife during a row at their home was given a conditional discharge by Tunbridge Wells magistrates last week. He was told that had the victim not been his wife the penalty might have been more severe."

Kent and Sussex Courier

The girls were mistaken for boys by police, the court heard, and when making the order the chairman of the bench told the 16-year-old that with care she could be "attractive to members of the opposite sex, who at the moment you hold no interest to."

The Leeds Stipendiary Magistrate Mr. F. D. L. Loy asked a probation officer to speak to Brown saying: "I am thinking about a community service order. It used to be said that scrubbing floors could help a pregnancy."

Yorkshire Evening Post

Judge Sir Harold Cassel QC told her: "If you were a man I would send you to jail without hesitation."

Newham Recorder

MR JUSTICE JUPP told him: "There are many times, even in a normal marriage, when a man wishes he could get rid of his wife, but I have to send you to prison because you killed a woman at the prime of her life."

Yorkshire Evening Press

"THERE were photographic sessions with topless models, and a number of strippers, two of whom took men from the audience and took their clothes off. The licensee and the organiser were charged with holding an indecent exhibition for gain. They were found not guilty on the judge's directions. But three girls were found guilty of committing an act outraging public decency."

South London Press

In Court

One advertisement was for a magazine called "Women and Animals" said Mr Beale. "What is that but an invitation to the most disgusting debasement of man and of animals?" he said.

Chief prosecutor in obscenity case, quoted in the Cambridge Evening News.

 ★ ★ ★

GIRL BEATEN TO DEATH WITH ARTIFICIAL LEG

A drunken construction worker has been found guilty of culpable homicide at Malemsbury, South Africa, for beating his girlfriend to death with his artificial leg. Ngxekese Simeno was given a two-year suspended sentence.

He said he would never use the leg, which was broken in the attack as a weapon again and was also finished with women as "they only cause trouble." Simeno's employers said they would repair his leg free of charge.—U.P.I.

Daily Telegraph.

★ ★ ★

She was threatened with violence before the man, reported to be aged 28 to 31, raped her.

He fled after stealing a small amount of property.

Detective Superintendent Ken Pickavance said: "This was a serious incident but fortunately the woman was not injured.

Liverpool Echo.

 ★ ★ ★

She was punched in the side of her face, dragged screaming to the ground by her hair and pulled along the street, while passers-by and four men in a nearby garage stood and watched because they "thought the man was her husband."

Worcester Evening News.

 ★ ★ ★

A 28-YEAR-OLD Greek baker was jailed for four months for misleading police, after claiming he was a burglar when arrested in an apartment block wearing only his underpants. It was later proved he was only stealing someone's wife.

Daily Telegraph.

"A YOUTH raped a 26-year-old woman over the bonnet of his car. After he was caught and bailed, he took another girl to the same area and indecently assulted her. Mr. Adrian Palmer, defending, said the offences ranked low in the calibre of rape offences and both girls were unharmed. And he said they had both contributed by allowing themselves to be driven off at night . . ."

Gloucester County Gazette.

"HE was cleared of rape after telling the jury that the 23-year-old divorcee consented to intercourse after he had burst into the refuge and dragged her upstairs to an attic."

Daily Telegraph.

The girl said he made her undress and have sex after threatening to kill her if she resisted.
Later he made love to her again.

The Sun.

If after four years fighting a barbarous enemy the Red soldier could be accused of nothing more than rape and watch stealing; then he was a relatively benevolent conqueror.

Edurance and Endeavour, Russian History 1812-1971 by J.L. Westwood, Oxford University Press.

RAPE . . . is when a man takes a woman sexually by force. Fortunately it is very rare, and even when it does happen it is often because a girl has "led a man on."

Handbook for Girls, by Anne Allan.

Home Office officials say there are about 1,700 rapes and more than 11,000 sex attacks each year, not including any offences of robbery or violence.

Leicester Mercury.

Out of Court

She carried on walking but the youth followed her and forced her into another alley where he raped her. The girl, who was West Indian, was not a virgin,

Would the Fund go out looking for projects which might need help?

'We're going to be a little bit feminine in this respect,' replied Charteris. 'Like a woman, we want to be attacked.'

Lord Charteris, provost of Eton, on the National Heritage Memorial Fund, quoted in the Observer.

★ ★ ★

"NO ONE denies that the Vikings enjoyed their own share of rape and pillage in an age when it was common-place; but it should not be forgotten that the difference between rape and seduction is only one of technique."

Magnus Magnusson writing in Popular Archaeology magazine.

Woman executed

TEHERAN, Saturday. — A woman and ten men were shot today for their part in an alleged plot to restore to power the Shah's last premier, now exiled in Paris.

At Camberwell, senior detectives were questioning three men and a blonde to find out who the torso victim was—

all of them have told me: "You can't swing a cat in the bedrooms."

It always creases me when I hear them say it for I always get a mental picture of the scene.

Now if they were swinging their wives by the hair, I could understand the sense to it because it would give them a pretty exact measurement and at the same time show her who was the boss.

Glasgow Evening Times.

A DOG, a woman, and a walnut tree. The more you beat them the better they are.

Geoffrey Smith, Gardeners World, BBC 2

★ ★ ★

"EVERY WOMAN loves the idea of a sheikh carrying her off on his white horse and raping her in his tent. It's a basic feminine instinct."

Omar Sharif, quoted in the Daily Mail

Picture House manager Robin Garrett, who moved the demonstrators from the front of the cinema, said: "As long as men and women have existed, women have been raped. It is nothing to do with films, it is to do with hormones."

Stafford Newsletter.

The Prime Minister

"HITHERTO, it has been easy to regard Mrs. Thatcher as the only man in her Cabinet. On the evidence of her little local reshuffle, and the great difficulty she apparently experienced in bringing herself to do it, she begins to look like the only woman after all."

Spectator

Mrs Thatcher and her bold, new policies are the only hope for our country. But confidence in her and her policies is being undermined by unemployment figures that seem frightening but in fact are phoney. out of 2·1 million unemployed. no less than about 659,000 — or just over one-third — were women.

Iain Sproat MP, Sunday Express

"HER HAIR newly done, Mrs. Thatcher had no apology for her war on public spending or for the Tories' crackdown on union power or the policy of returning some of State industry to private hands."

Yorkshire Evening Press.

"MRS THATCHER seemed anxious to voice a view on the new bilious phone booth (and what woman could resist having the last word on decor?) But she made a firm effort and restrained herself."

Andrew Alexander, Daily Mail.

The Lord Mayor's Banquet (BBC1, 10.55pm). Dear old Mrs Thatcher tries to rally the country in her speech. The poor thing looks a little peeky what with the cares of office. She is certainly putting on weight. Can't she see how unfeminine it is getting mixed up in what is really men's work after all? I shouldn't let my wife go to one of these City dinners.

Catholic Herald.

William: What do you want to be when you grow up?
Thomas: I think I'll be the Prime Minister.
William: Don't be stupid! Only girls can be Prime Minister!

Overheard in Bognor Regis.

"It was a messy business and something that only a woman could clear up. I believe that under the same circumstances all the other Prime Ministers would hve swept it under the carpet."

Andrew Boyle, quoted in the Evening Standard

"THE NEAREST we have come to a really modern memorial for women is a plaque in West London, to the memory of old Mother Riley. But this music hall character was, of course, a male in drag. Which, when you come to think about it, is what most of our famous women look like . . ."

Kenneth Robinson in High-life magazine.

Mr. Stokes: What view does my right hon. Friend take of the United Nations conference on women, which is being held in Copenhagen at a cost of £1½ millions? We have sent 10 delegates to that conference. Will the conference help her and other women?

The Prime Minster: I rather think we made it before that conference took place.

The time was going quickly and she had to be at a meeting in the Cabinet room.

What was the proudest moment of her life? The woman in Maggie might have said it was the day she married Denis, or had the twins. But it was the Prime Minister in her who answered

South Wales Echo.

"WHAT IS remarkable about the Prime Minister is her inconsistencies . . . In short, as one elderly Tory MP was heard to remark, having a woman leader is like being at home all day."

Julian Critchley MP writing in the Listener.

Her attractiveness misleads people and sometimes disguises her ability to hard political infighting.

Simon Hoggart, the Guardian.

Have the Tories even been more vulnerable to ridicule?

Record unemployment, unstoppable inflation, unintelligible economics, disillusioned voters, nuclear bomb rattling and biggest joke of all, a woman Prime Minister!"

London Evening Standard

At least Mrs THATCHER must from now on be seen, not just as a woman surprisingly holding down the job, but as a driving force in Europe.

Politics

City Recorder
CENTRAL LONDON'S LOCAL NEWSPAPER

LADY
COUNCILMAN
SLAMS
CITY MALE
DOMINATION

Mr Suthee said that corruption in Thailand has three root causes: legal loopholes, power abuse and bad wives.

New Sunday Times, Kuala Lumpur.

NOW that her husband has been elected leader of the Labour Party, Jill Craigie might just become Mrs Jill Foot.

Daily Mail.

"As Mrs Foot waited to hear her husband's fate, she did what most women would do in the circumstances, and had her hair done."

Daily Telegraph.

The draft constitution terms will reflect the following principles of party organization: All voting will be on the principle of "one man one vote".

The Times reporting the Social Democrat launch.

IT IS RECKONED to be twenty times or more difficult for a woman, Labour or Tory to be selected as it is for a man. The reason is simple: women are catty about voting for a woman and men do not much want to be represented by a "skirt".

Sir Gerald Nabarro's autobiography NAB 1.

My wife covered her face during the sodomy scene; but I didn't walk out because I thought there might be a message for me

Sir Horace Cutler, leader of the Greater London Council, quoted in the Sunday Times on The Romans in Britain.

MR BOTTOMLEY, who has been an MP in Middlesbrough for nearly 20 years, says he is stepping down to let new young blood take over. "I want to have an opportunity of getting a young man in," he said.

Middlesbrough Evening Gazette.

Despite the antagonism which Mr Reagan has unexpectedly provoked by his views on women's rights and abortion, women will still be fairly represented on the floor of the convention, making up 40 per cent of the state delegations.

The Guardian

★ ★ ★

LABOUR PARTY.—At the annual meeting of the Barton and District Branch Labour Party the secretary reported a good year. After the election of the officers for 1981/82, coffee was served by the women.

Cambridgeshire Weekly News.

we mustn't for a single moment forget the wonderful women — wives, secretaries and even the ladies who hand round tea at local party meetings – who enable us to lead the life of a politician."

Clement Freud quoted in Woman's World magazine.

"AND sitting among it all the most beauteous wife in all British politics, Mrs Neil Kinnock, a school teacher whose pupils I can only envy with a sort of besotted wistfulness. Her Lord, Mr Neil Kinnock himself, started the lapel badge wearing craze here . . ."

Christopher Jones on Today Radio 4.

IN the back of most women's minds there is a deep, smouldering resentment against the Common Market. They know little about it but they blame the EEC for what they consider to be the high price of food. And food is their business.

★ ★ ★

"THERE ARE two ways you can approach this . . . One is to say that those bright boys who do their O levels and A levels and end with a degree in physics will decide what our nuclear power programme is to be . . .

Tony Benn speaking to the National Association of Environmental Education.

★ ★ ★

In the last three weeks he has acquired the information he needs to prove what he calls " an act of sabotage designed to prevent their own incompetence being shown up." At a conference tomorrow on " Getting Britain Moving," he will itemise the whole thing. He tells me that in one region " a single solitary spinster " was sent out to examine the cuts that were possible in six counties. She was given a fortnight to do it and not surprisingly found very little that could be cut.

QUEEN AMINA habitually took new lovers wherever she stopped during her wars and had them disposed of when she left. She is fondly remembered as "a woman as capable as a man".

From the Republic of Nigeria calendar.

★ ★ ★

QUEEN ELIZABETH had long outlived men's affection if not their fear and respect and after fifty years of petticoat government they welcomed a male ruler, and the end of female trantrums, sulks, and irrationality

Stuart England, by J. P. Kenyon (Penguin).

The CND Easter marches from the Aldermaston nuclear research centre were not only extremely well behaved: they were also somehow typically English.

Primus stoves were lit in schoolhalls, sleeping-bags also were spread therein and sometimes, for the fortunate girl nuclear disarmer, Mr Right put in his appearance.

Alan Watkins, The Listener

★ ★ ★

IF COUNCIL tenants cannot afford the 82p a week rent increase introduced by the council in November, then they should get rid of their "TVs, flashy cars and women." Tory councillor Chris Clark told Thursday's council meeting.

Middlesex Advertiser and Gazette.

★ ★ ★

MR PETER TAPSELL, MP discussed import penetration. "We are like the woman in the hay field who lay on her back and shouted rape, rape, rape all summer long."

Conservative Central Office news service.

"A LABOUR move to give extra cash aid to Warrington's Refuge for Battered Wives was defeated . . . Councillor Denis Chapman (Conservative) said: 'I think is is always a good rule never to encourage the break-up of a marriage. If we provide somewhere for these women to go they will run there without a second thought . . .' "

Warrington Guardian.

Mrs Silkin had been divorced a year from the film director, Hugh Russell Lloyd when she met John Silkin, then a young solicitor. They married two months later.

She had not relished giving up what was turning out to be a promising film career. "But John did not want me to work. He likes me to be there when he comes home.

Mrs ZITA KELLY, who from today is Lady Provost of Glasgow, came across in her interview with my colleague Jessica Barrett yesterday as a quiet, gentle, self-effacing person with little interest in politics.

And these are indeed pleasing qualities in a woman.

Charles Graham, "Scotland's most penetrating writer," in the Glasgow Evening Times.

it is harder for a woman to get through selection procedures and to be accepted as a competent politician than it is for her male counterpart.

This theory is obviously not without its element of truth— there are some obvious prejudices—as witnessed by the local Tory party who believed that a male candidate was preferable because "if you have a man you get two for the price of one"

AN EXTREME example is the gunning down of Bernadette Devlin. An appalling event. But a fearful reminder of what may befall women when they thrust themselves into the frontline.

Slough Observer.

The World of Sport

TENNIS: David Irvine at Wimbledon

Mother's day at last

The Guardian.

BEFORE a backhand once again becomes something administered by the little woman for reading at the breakfast table, a few reflections on the Wimbledon experience.

Hugh Keevins, The Scotsman

> The two players were off court for 61 minutes during which Mrs. Cawley showered changed her clothes and had what every mother enjoys; a cup of tea.

Yorkshire Post.

★ ★ ★

His new acquisitions of a wife and county captaincy have given him a secure platform on which to base this final fling of his Test career.

The Observer

> Susan, who says she isn't trying to strike a blow for women's lib, was praised by Phil Head, a member of last year's winning Oxford crew.
> "She's a tough little miss," he said. "We regard her as just another male cox."

Daily Mirror.

THE DANGER is with Evonne that sometimes she starts humming to herself, thinking of the baby at home, and the family.

Fred Perry, Radio 2.

★ ★ ★

> WHEN Martina Navratilova plays at Wimbledon this week, the eye of every healthy lusty male will be on her.
> She personifies the essence of attractive femininity.
> Disillusioning, isn't it, to learn that she is shacked up in the United States with the country's most aggressive lesbian?
> I sigh with nostalgia, for the day when at tournaments like Wimbledon the greatest danger to the chastity of young lady tennis stars came from randy males.
> Devastating, isn't it, to learn that nowadays their greatest peril would seem to come from other lassies in frilly panties?

Sir John Junor, Sunday Express

> He tried to smear it, had his middle stump knocked out, gave Willis a deserved fourth wicket and the ladies among the largest of the three crowds a dismissal they could understand.

Robin Marlar, Sunday Times.

Roger Cawley's role, on the surface, is a faintly embarrassing one. He is a tennis husband and the Women's Tennis Association guidebook explains his function thus- 'Roger, once a tournament player himself, practises with Evonne and often warms her up for her matches.'

The Observer.

In September, more fortunate county cricketers are weighing up the options of that coaching job in Johannesburg or grade cricket in Sydney; or Christmas at home for a change, to get more mileage out of the wife and the V-reg Saab.

Scyld Berry, The Observer.

WOMEN'S FOOTBALL

Interested?

Contact
EDGWARE LADIES' FOOTBALL CLUB

Managers: Brian Booth, 958-9148; Peter Harrigan, 952-5417

Hendon Times

"I REMEMBER sending my wife to the supermarket early so that we'd have everything done in time to sit down and watch the Cup Final . . ."

Lawrie McMenemy quoted in Radio Times.

FIFA, under its egregious President Jose Havelange, has duly cheapened and extended the World Cup, which might just as well now be described as the World and his Wife Cup, so easy has it become for a second rate competitor to qualify.

Brian Glanville, World Soccer magazine.

NOW how absurd to dare suggest
A female could become a ref;
It's bad enough with sponsored shirts
Without officials wearing skirts.

Southampton football programme

"I think it is distasteful. I like women in their proper place, nicely dressed and showing themselves off. It is totally unpalatable to see them wrestling."

Scarborough councillor Jack Smith on women wrestlers, Norther Echo.

"ISN'T one of the main features of football match attendance still that it enables men to get away from nagging wives . . .?"

Portsmouth manager Frank Burrows.

★ ★ ★

 Ideally, if dining space allows, then ladies should be invited. Apart from the fact that they decorate the occasion, we rely on them as occasional beaters.

Shooting Times and Country Magazine

WILL YOU PLEASE make a special effort to decorate your house/street/dog/wife this year it makes so much difference to the atmosphere.

Chairman's notes, Fowey Royal Regatta souvenir booklet.

★ ★ ★

"OFFICERS of the day are reminded that their wives or girlfriends are expected to serve in the tea bar."

Spotted on a sailing club noticeboard.

★ ★ ★

 On no account consider taking along wives or mistresses. Women can be admirable creatures in their own way but the female who is content to pull your trolley for 36 holes a day without speaking, without deserting to the shops, without wanting to pinch the car for excursions to the beach, without complaining about the service and without generally fouling up a golf trip has not been born.

Peter Dobereiner, the Guardian.

In the words of one bachelor player who makes his thousand runs a year: 'I'd make 2,000 a year if I had a wife behind me — someone to encourage, wash socks and come home to in the evening instead of drinking at the bar with the lads and ending up at the late-night take-away.'

The Observer

SUE LONGDEN, of Essex Ladies Athletic Club, made it a great week for her husband and coach, Bruce, by winning the Women's Three A's Championship and Olympic Pentathlon Trial at Birmingham.

The Observer.

The Scotsman

The World of Medicine

"DESPITE the fact that women are significantly different from men, there is considerable reproductive evidence that they belong to the same species."

British Medical Journal.

★ ★ ★

"IT'S SO different from looking into cars or throats, handling distasteful skin diseases or trying to persuade hysterical women they haven't got cancer."

Forty Years Of Murder by pathologist Professor Keith Simpson

THE inaugural meeting of the Lymm branch of the Muscular Dystrophy Group of Great Britain was held last week. The following members were elected as office bearers: Mr. D. Webster, chairman; Mr. G. Gleave, vice-chairman; Mr. R. Davis, secretary and Mr. I. Davis, secretary and Mr. I McGuire, treasurer. Several of the women members volunteered for administration duties.

Warrington Guardian.

Geriatrics offers a rewarding career for the woman doctor.

BMA News Review

Said Mr Empson: "With more female promiscuity, and pre - marital experiences, women expect orgasms and more successful sex relationships.

"When they sometimes do not achieve this satisfaction, they start complaining. This can give their men partners sex problems."

Brighton Evening Argus.

★ ★ ★

"Males are more active in seeking sexual stimuli in the environment, and if as a result of early learning, adolescent knockbacks, or inferiority feelings arising from any source, women become classified as unapproachable, they will turn to near approximations of women, e.g. : children, underwear, sheep, rubber blow-ups . . ."

Glenn Wilson, British Journal of Sexual Medicine.

★ ★ ★

DR WILKINSON dispells the myth that migraine sufferers are mainly to be found among the intellectual elite and says that in fact, migraine is about three times more common in women than men.

Sunderland Echo review of a Family Doctor booklet on migraine.

Our wish, as surgeons — husbands and fathers ourselves — is to preserve the life of other men's wives.

F. D. Skidmore, writing about mastectomy, Sunday Times

"IN THE premenstrual phase women may be irritable, angry and emotionally labile. During the postmenstrual phase, however, they float through life, wafted along on a tide of hormones, euphoric, placid and tolerant, womanly in every way."

Dr Peter Martin, Pulse magazine.

BOSSES at a Port Glasgow factory are to-day trying to trace the cause of a mystery illness which floored the women workers.
A doctor who examined the workers said:
"Of course it could have been a bout of mass hysteria — remembering that not a man in the factory was affected."

Evening Times.

"IF you're a girl, I hope you'll be beautiful, because a beautiful girl can make somebody very happy . . .
If you're a boy, I hope you'll be strong and courageous."

From a BMA Family Doctor pamphlet, The Facts of Life for Children by Roger Pilkington.

"BATTERED divorcees tend to turn their new, placid husbands into wife beaters."

Dr John Williamson, Doctor magazine.

"WOMEN can be as intelligent as men.
They are certainly as competent and efficient in administration and organisation, if they are given the opportunities and training. There are not so many women with unusal qualities of genius, initiative and originality as there are men, but this is compensated by the fact that there are fewer women with evil and criminal impulses. Women and girls need to be treated as rational beings. The more they are treated in this way, the more they will respond . . .
Some writers have represented women as being like a liquid, which takes the shape of any vessel into which it is poured. This is too cynical, but there is an element of truth in it."

From a BMA Family Doctor pamphlet 15+ Facts of Life by Kenneth Barnes.

Are you satisfied with her breasts?
If not – why not buy her an Aquamaid?

Health and Strength magazine.

A TAXI DRIVER is over-weight and suffers spells of dizziness while driving. In the final incident, which involves a runaway pram, he meets his nemesis. This is a film about obesity suitable for slimming clubs, women's groups etc.

From a film summary sent to schools by Trafford area health authority.

★ ★ ★

The only male voice on tape was Dr. Crowhurst — we thought this would add weight and importance to the dangers of smoking in pregnancy.

Article on ante-natal health education in Bridge, the newspaper for Health Service staff.

★ ★ ★

"TO ATTAIN tolerable competence takes 15 minutes: novices should experiment on wife or girlfriend."

Dr James Cyriax on manipulation, in Pain Topics magazine.

★ ★ ★

A NUMBER of economic and institutional measures are proposed to encourage people to have only one child, even if that child is a girl.

Scientific American report on China's polulation plans.

AND one of our guests, retired surgeon Jessica Goldsmith, is going to tell us when is a doctor a Dr. and when is he a Mr.

Sue Lawley on Midweek, Radio 4.

7. What about your appearance?

a) I feel ugly and unfeminine. I'm □
   depressed and hide in the house
   all day.

b) I take pride in my appearance. I □
   choose attractive maternity-wear,
   bathe and wash my hair regularly,
   and still wear make-up.

c) A constant stream of Romeos □
   serenade me day and night.

Your score.

1) a—0, b—1, c—3, 2) a—3, b—2, c—0. 3) a—2, b—1, c—3, d—0
4) a—0, b—3, c—0. 5) a—3, b—0, c—3. 6) a— See your doctor,
b—0, c—3, d—0. 7) a—0, b—3, c—0.

ARE YOU HELPING YOUR BABY'S CHANCES?

West Midlands Health Service Ad. Birmingham Evening Mail

LADIES
ARE NOT ALLOWED
INSIDE THE
HOSPITAL

Sandown racecourse.

World Medicine

MARCH 21, 1981

This year's good reason for joining the BMA

Primary Education

WHEN Susie was a Junior,
A Junior Susie was
She went "Miss, Miss, I can't
do this, I've got my
knickers in a twist."
When Susie was a mummy,
A mummy Susie was
She went cook, cook, cook,
cook.
When Susie was a granny,
A granny Susie was
She went knit, knit, knit
knit.

*Heard in an infant's
playground.*

★ ★ ★

When Susy was a teenager
A teenager Susy was
She said
Ooh arr I've lost my bra
I've left my knickers in my
Boyfriend's car.

Sung in the playground.

★ ★ ★

"CLAP hands for Daddy to
come,
Daddy has money and
Mummy has none."

*Forty Favourite Nursery
Rhymes, Macdonald
Educational.*

"BOYS especially need someone masculine with whom they
can be rough and get dirty . . .
For a girl, father plays a
different but equally important
role. From him she learns to gain
confidence in herself as a
female, and it does not take her
long to discover the rewards of
fluttering her lashes."

*Toddler's Progress, by Mrs.
Georgina Mallalieu, Mrs Avril
Rodway, and Mrs June
Weatherall, published by
Bounty Publications.*

★ ★ ★

" IF PARENTS really believe
the answer is No to sex until
the age of 16 is reached they
should enforce it with par-
ental discipline and if necessary lock up their wayward
daughters."

*Letter from Dr Adrian Rogers,
vice-chairman of Responsibility
In Welfare in the Daily Telegraph.*

★ ★ ★

Fisher Price Tool Kit
*A twenty three piece toy includes wind-up drill
and attachments that can be used to assemble
a three- piece work bench with nuts and bolts
provided. Give him his own tool kit just like Dads.*

Fisher Price Kitchen Set
*Twenty-four piece play set complete with mini -
cooker – just the thing for the little miss.*

"ALL THE Daddies on the
bus go read, read, read . . .
All the Mummies on the bus
go chatter, chatter,
chatter . . ."

*Song taught in Bristol
nursery school.*

The idea was to get the children involved in the exercise by getting them to go through the motions of crossing properly. The girls pushed the prams over the crossing while the boys drove the cars.

Richmond and Kew Herald.

★ ★ ★

'DON'T WORRY, said Dick, with a grin. "Anne has been at work — you know how she loves to put everything in its place . . ."

"All the same, George will have to help me," said Anne firmly. "I don't expect boys to tidy up and cook and do things like that — but George ought to because she's a girl."

"If only I had been born a boy," groaned George.

Five Have a Wonderful Time, by Enid Blyton.

Secondary Education

A boy's sure instinct is not to do anything which girls are supposed to do. A girl's sure instinct is to play at being mother.

George Gale, Daily Express.

A GROUP of fathers claim their sons are being turned into cissies by school needlework and cookery classes.

One father, Mr Tony James, an engineer, of Eshe Road, Crosby, said: "I think boys should be taught subjects, and not lessons for girls. I am concerned at the effect these classes could have

Daily Telegraph.

"FEW GOOD, full-length, new fairy tales, or honest-to goodness children's novels, get published. What's to be done? Mr Goldthwaite is ready with more answers than the abolition of awards. Sack the overload of women who have dominated the hen-pecked world of children's book publishing for half a century — their rule has been characterised by timidity, domesticity, schmaltz for the tinies, women's libbery and bogus realism for the teens, Remember the unthinkable: almost all good children's books have been written by men."

Book Review in The Economist

IN the third forms you will be able to do two technical/domestic subjects. The following will be offered — needlework, cookery, woodwork, metalwork, applied science and technology.

All the girls are advised to do needlework.

Circular to pupils at a Harpenden school.

"WHAT IS the similarity between a bus, a woman and a new idea in geography?

ANSWER: none are worth chasing because another will soon come along!"

Times Educational Supplement.

BEATRICE would be a person, not a shadow, she would keep her independence, and it must be remembered that loyalty and independence may march side by side. A woman who values her independence is usually loyal to the man who gives it her.

From Pan Study Aid to Much Ado About Nothing.

CHOOSING the type of work you want to do can be the second most important decision of your life (the most important is, of course, choosing your husband).

Handbook for Girls.

Further Education

Bangor Technical College offers everything from angling to wood carving and yoga and one obviously for women called "Making the best of yourself!"

Belfast Telegraph

★ ★ ★

"I AM sorry to see that the Gazette has succumbed to the current use of 'Ms' to indicate the female of the species in its Student Lists and Examination Results etc. As probably they are almost 100 per cent single, it is quite likely they would prefer to be known as such (and therefore 'available'!)"

Letter from Peter Readings in Guy's Hospital magazine.

★ ★ ★

WE WELCOMED the 70 incoming male undergraduates and the 42 women, at a freshmen's dinner . . . According to the most experienced observers, this proportion of men to women is likely to persist, being the normal one.

The Warden, writing in the Wadham College Gazette.

★ ★ ★

"THE undermentioned gentlemen have permission to occupy rooms as stated. Name: Miss J. I. Elliot Miss K. R. Batty, Miss K. A. Hagan, Miss J. E. Bendor-Samuel . . ."

Notice posted in Christ Church College, Oxford.

THE FIRST batch of highly qualified entrants into the course consisted of 24 pretty women and one very happy-looking man.

Principal's report, University of Glasgow.

"IN SPITE of the fact that most candidates were girls, the maths and science results were excellent."

Report by J. Almond of the Academic Board meeting at Hardenhuish School, Chippenham, Wilts.

"THE WIFE of a student will normally be admitted for the period of her husband's authorised stay without restriction on taking employment . . .
"The husband of a student will need to qualify for entry in his own right and will not normally be granted leave to remain solely because his wife is studying in the UK. If full-time employment is required a work permit must be obtained.

Leaflet from the United Kingdom Council for Overseas Student Affairs.

Now there's a profound thought; is the OU feminine or masculine? I think it's a woman. It likes to dress up for degree ceremonies and is bitchy about those who don't wear the correct dress. It also sulks when you criticise it.

Sean Ward in Sesame, the Open University newspaper.

A BURNLEY-BASED company has created a first class career appointment for a person experienced in Female Control, also experience in Hand and Machine production.

Burnley Express

FOR THE SAKE of clarity, and to retain the "personal touch" the female gender has generally been adopted in any reference to welfare officers, and the male gender elsewhere.

Civil Service Department guide.

Making the Most of Human Resources — a workshop for men who manage women, Uxbridge, Middlesex July 16-17 Fee: £125.

Financial Times.

⋆ ⋆ ⋆

"A PREPONDERANCE of female or youthful labour, where a natural irresponsibility is difficult to control, is another unfavourable aspect of the management of hands."

Chartered Insurance Institute tuition manual.

"TO KEEP costs down, cheap docile labour is necessary so young women provide the answer."

Judy Cox on making microprocessors, Computing magazine.

"MANAGEMENT is a word that only makes sense when the man comes first."

British Airway's cabin crew journal, Contact.

PROBLEMS OF MANNER

A Male Officer Loses his Temper: Should he become emotional, angry or abusive, it is best simply to listen patiently. Do not argue or show disapproval. Be sure to let the officer know that his loss of temper is not a permanent black mark against him.
A Female Officer Becomes Distressed and Weeps: Try to assess why it has happened. Is she upset because she has not been able to cope with the work problems being dicussed? Sympathetic looks and gestures rather than words are called for.

Instructions for job assessment interviews. Department of Employment.

Music & Video Week Yearbook 1981

WHERE WOULD YOU LOOK FOR A LIBERATED LADY?

NOT IN A BOARDROOM — NOT IN A JET PLANE
but in a correctly designed and beautifully fitted kitchen

Advertisement in the Wokingham Times

IN ORDER to assist us in our efforts to keep the Private Trade Days as genuine business occasions, I would ask you to ensure that tickets are used only by persons who have a serious professional interest in the aerospace industry. Unless they can comply with the aforementioned requirements, it will not be possible for the Society to accommodate ladies on the Trade Days.

The Society of British Aero-space Companies in a circular to members about Farn-borough Air Show.

"NOTWITHSTANDING the enlargement of women's status. . . the presumption in law is that she is incapable of understanding a business trans-action by the exercise of her own wit."

Studies In Practical Banking, by R. W. Jones.

RECOGNITION came in the end. In 1951 she was made deputy clerk of the council and when she married the clerk, Mr John Shaw, five years later, it looked as if she had well and truly arrived.

July issue of Public Service and Local Government Journal.

 ★ ★ ★

ORGANISED and sponsored by the fashion house Butte Knit the competition is designed to spotlight the new breed of highly successful women executives. Points in the final, which will take the form of individual interviews, will be awarded for grooming and appearance.

Press Release from Butte Knit announcing the finals of its Female Executive of the Year competition.

★ ★ ★

You might wear a skirt but we'll ask you to do a man's job.

Ad. by Western Automobile Co., The Scotsman.

MR GOULDEN went on to ask his audience to consider the introduction of a type of "ancillary" — married women who could take on routine work in the office and free journalists for more important tasks.

UK Press Gazette

★ ★ ★

A SECOND YOUNG LADY, aged 25-35, required as senior consultant/instructor for Huddersfield branch of Bob Sweeneys Olympic Figure and Fitness Club.

Earnings in excess of £3,000 pa for right applicant.

YOUNG MAN, aged 25-35, required as senior consultant/instructor for Huddersfield branch of Bob Sweeney's Olympic Figure and Fitness Club.

Earnings in excess of £3,500 pa for right applicant.

Huddersfield Examiner.

An interesting vacancy exists for an
Attractive Young
G I R L
or
Ambitious Y O U T H

Manchester Evening News.

COUNTER HAND

for Hertford betting office. Interesting work in friendly clean shop. Experience not essential.
Suitable 'mum' or person
Requiring 3/4 afternoons per week.

★ ★ ★

CITY OF LIVERPOOL
Social Services Department
SENIOR HOUSEFATHER
£5,178-£6,132
HOUSEMOTHER
£3,609-£5,325

★ ★ ★

Assistant
Manageress (m/f)
FOR THE
LONDON DUNGEON

★ ★ ★

THE CLUB and Institute Union require a Caretaker and Wife. Duties to include responsibility for security, opening and closing the building, supervision of contract cleaners and to undertake handyman tasks (wife to make tea).

Islington Gazette.

We know the person we are looking for is probably quite rare, which is why we will offer an above average renumeration package. We also know he or she might be hiding away somewhere not realising their potential, but we'll get our man.

Sit. vac. advertisement in Audio-Visual Magazine.

"A PATENT may be obtained by:
A sole inventor,
Joint inventors
A miscellaneous group including
(a) an infant,
(b) a woman,
(c) an alien.

DIRECT discrimination arises when a person treats a woman, in any circumstances relevant for the purposes of the Act, less favourably on the grounds of her sex than he treats, or would treat, a man.

Equal Opportunities Commission booklet.

Evening Standard.

I REGRET to have to answer your letter negatively, but . . . we do not have a vacancy. Even if we did have a vacancy, we would most likely award the post to a Miss or Mrs., but not to a Ms.

Letter from Alan Armstrong, of Alan Armstrong Associates (booksellers) to . . Ms. W. A. Beecher

Business News: Secretaries

The course at Evesham College of Further Education included instructions on filling in petty cash vouchers and arranging flowers in executives' offices. Women clerks were advised how to apply lipstick "to correct the shape of the mouth and add charm to the face."

Mr Patrick Rust, the council's chief executive, said: "We thought it would have been advantageous for this employee, at her advanced age, to be included in this course but she did not feel she should go.

Daily Telegraph report of the case of a clerk who faced a council disciplinary committee after refusing to take the course.

I want him to like me... now I've got him the wrong number again...

The Post Office's Telecoms magazine.

"Secretaries were beginning to wobble rather than wiggle. The competition will make the scenery more pleasant for the men."

Participant in the Manchester Co-op slimming competition, Daily Star.

IT'S EVERY typist's dream to wake up to a Prince's kiss. Trying to keep one million typists and their mums happy may at least be some sort of compensation for near celibacy.

Michael De La Noy on Prince Charles's love life. Forum magazine.

> "STATIC can also build up in the body whilst sitting in the office chair, so girls save the wiggle for walking."

Surrey County Council safety handout.

★ ★ ★

> "WE'RE not too keen on supporting teenage-girl type sewing-machine projects. . ."

Patrick Naylor, chief executive of BSC (Industry) talking about attracting industry to towns hit by steel closures. Metal and Materials magazine.

"THEY MADE ME DO IT!"

I'm seventeen. I'm a receptionist at a jingle company.

I'll admit I'm quite round and full-breasted for my age.

I even overheard one of my bosses say I have a nice little bum.

But that's no reason for them to make me do all those, well, *things*.

Like the other night in the office when we all had lots of funny drinks and I had something called a stinger and we all had to dance around and kiss everybody.

Just because the advertising agency phoned up and said 'We love the jingle'.

Or the night they made me dress up like a duck and go quack-quack just because another agency phoned up and said they 'got the account' and the music was 'wonderful'. I had a stinger that night, too.

And then there was the night they won those dumb awards. Over at the Hilton.

They made me put them on my desk.

The awards, I mean.

And later, when that big man, Mr. Bindley I think his name was, caught me upstairs by the drinks cabinet. It was dark and I was scared. He said I was a naughty girl and deserved a little spanking.

But that's another confession.

★ ★ ★

Business News: Finance

MORE women going out to work and neglecting the housework could be the cause of a massive outbreak of fleas in Worthing.

Worthing Gazette.

The salary survey carried out by the Institute of Quantity Surveyors uncovered a wide disparity in the earnings as between sexes. The median basic salary of the female comes out at £5967 against the male's £7000.

What can be the reason? Peter South, IQS director, rightly pointed out that there was a much smaller sample of women (27) than men (2660) and that this could have distorted the figures. Part of the answer, he suggested, might also be that women were not as good as men.

"A WIFE plays a vitally important role in the running of a home. She does the cooking, the shopping, the washing, nurses the children, and may even do a part time job as well."

Prudential Insurance leaflet.

BUSINESSMEN do not yet appreciate what their wives are really worth, but they are learning fast. Besides taking care of the office chores, your wife can be a tax saver provided she is on the regular payroll.

Sunday Times.

'I have had to sell one or two paintings but I haven't yet been reduced to sending my wife out to work,'

Financier Richard Tarling quoted in the Daily Mail.

Mr. Sandy Brigstocke told the committee that parents helped out and filled the gap for teachers at primary school level. "If women are made redundant they might be able to go home and look after their husbands and children better," he said.

Surrey Advertiser.

"'THE 'fit' between the money supply and the cost of living exists, but it is rather loose and a bit baggy. Like a 32A girl wearing a 36C, things tend to jiggle around quite a bit."

Money, by Lawrence S. Ritter and William L. Silber.

We are looking at the question of keeping families together', he said. 'Would it be possible for instance for the chief executive's wife to be trained as a teleprinter operator?"

Eric Willcock, Emergency Planning Officer, West Midlands County Council, on plans for equipping a war room bunker. The Observer.

TREAT each one of the shares you hold as a mistress. As long as she performs well, stick with her, but if she starts to falter and goes down when she should be going up, kick her out of bed and get another one.

Bob Beckman, LBC Radio,

 ★ ★ ★

his wife won't ring to ask where he has been because, in his words: "I caught her at 17 and I've trained her not to call unless there's a family crisis."

Harold Musgrove, managing director of Austin Morris, interviewed in the Birmingham Evening Mail.

Women: are they simply the people who help you make a living from your cookshop, and who make calendars more interesting? Or are they a vast, untapped source of profit, plucking up the courage to put those dust-gathering shelves up themselves?

Hardware Trades Journal.

★ ★ ★

Business News: Social Events

"IT CERTAINLY was a feast. The ladies sat down to four courses, the men to five . . ."

Victoria Mather reporting the Cutler's Feast, Sheffield Telegraph

"MAY I perhaps make a pleas to all those Tablers who have not allowed their wives to become involved in Circle. Please reconsider your position and let her find the friendship and fellowship in Circle that you fin in Table. Please consider letter her out once a fortnight. . ."

Letter from the Ladies Circle Area Chairman in Devon Round Table magazine, Colic.

"THE FINAL of the CBI/ Family Circle competition to find the 1981 housewife economic expert (known as the Queen Bee) will be held on Thursday."

CBI press release.

IT IS because these evenings — always black tie and men only occasions — offer such excellent, unique entertainment that I thought your Company would be interested in the Club's activities.

Letter from Henry Cooper, Chief Executive for Sport, World Sporting Club to Dr. E.H. Nelson, Chairman, Taylor Nelson and Associates (from Dr. Elizabeth H. Nelson)

"ONLY a few of the original wives' groups are still active and we have decided to re-launch our activities in the New Year. In keeping with our image we are changing the name of our group to the 'Chamber Maids'."

Highlights, Norwich Junior chamber of commerce

Should women be trained to use the fire equipment?
It is not essential that they be trained if there are always likely to be sufficient men available to deal with emergencies.

Fire Prevention, journal of the Fire Protection Society.

"I SHOULD explain that the event tends to be very much a male occasion. Freddie Truman is not known for his timidity and does not want to be accused of upsetting the fairer sex. Therefore, although ladies will be welcomed if they do turn up, it is felt that their presence may inhibit our after-lunch speaker which we would obviously like to avoid!"

Invitation - ITT sponsored Radio Industries Council Lunch

ALTHOUGH this is a professional function there is no embargo on ladies wishing to attend . . ."

Association of London Borough Planning Officers circular on its annual reception

The vicar, the Rev. Russell Owen, has had a spate of girls to baptise since 1978: "I have no idea of the reason for it. But perhaps it could be God's way of visiting his wrath on the church for refusing to ordain women."

Oliver Gillie, Sunday Times.

★ ★ ★

"MR BELL has now retired, and at a farewell he was presented with a cheque for £700 as a thank you gift from the two congregations. Mrs Bell was given an Electrolux vacuum cleaner".

The Unitarian magazine.

★ ★ ★

"IT WAS generally agreed that the exceptional turnout to the Men's Supper was entirely due to women — nagging wives to get us there, and a willing band of helpers to provide a tasty supper (and they even did the washing up!)"

Newsletter of All Saints Chuch , Laleham, Staines.

★ ★ ★

Home is where mother is and it is the special privilege of womanhood to provide that fostering care of husband and children that turns a mere dwelling into a home. When that is well done wifehood and motherhood come to their highest glory,

The Rev. Bernard Morgan, Lowestoft Journal.

Andrew and Peter are here, with James the Great and Bartholomew, and to show that heaven is unisex two unidentified female saints as well."

The Rector's guide to St. Andrew's Church, Castle Coombe, Wilts.

★ ★ ★

Belles of the village

I'm sure devout advocates of women's lib will be pleased at the growing success of the Kemerton handbell ringers. They are, of course, all ladies — Les Soeurs Jacquelines you might say. Fortunately they are kept in check by a male,

John Bright column, Birmingham Post.

There may be in the church some women who would fulfil the office of churchwarden with grace and energy, but while we have a fund of men who have discretion, who know their way round balance sheets, budgets, and banking, who are at home in such matters as downspouts and gutters, central heating and electrical systems, church fabric, furnishings, insurance, maintenance of churchyard equipment, why call on the ladies?

Flixton Parish Magazine.

"WE had imagined that the typewriter was masculine — steady, reliable, unflappable, firm as a rock. She has, of the last few days, shown herself to be feminine — temperamental, moody, one day up, the next day down, unreliable . . . look at your wife and that's our typewriter!"

Parish magazine of St Mark's, Dalston, London E8

Hindus are not permitted to utter a falsehood without sinning except in the following circumstances.
1. To secure an advantageous match.
2. To lure a woman to sexual intercourse.
3. To save one's own life.
4. To prevent total loss of wealth; and
5. To save a Brahmin.

Letter in The Times

"IT WILL require constant effort to maintain true contentment while so much is being said about 'women's liberation.' But are those who take the lead in this movement really contented? How can they be when they ignore the fact that the God-ordained role for a wife is that of a helper and complement, not that of a head or competitor? (Gen. 2 : 18)."

The Watchtower.

Kitchen Prayer

*Lord of pots and pans and things,
since I've not time to be*

*A saint by doing lovely things
or watching late with Thee*

*Or dreaming in the dawn light
or storming Heaven's gates,*

*Make me a saint by getting meals
and washing up the plates.*

Devotional card at Roman Catholic conference.

"ADAM'S Evening is strictly for the men of the church and their friends, so the ladies can take to their knitting in peace and quiet for an hour or so."

Caversham Hill Chapel newsletter.

". . . the new arrangement is primarily intended for the uninitiated reader who, understandably, is often put off by such mundane chapters as 'The Cow' or 'Women' . . ."

N.J. Darwood's introduction to Penguin Classics' Koran.

"WIVES be subject to your husbands as to the Lord. For the husband is the head of the wife, just as Christ is the head of the Church . . . As the Church is subject to Christ so must wives be to their husbands in everything."

Optional marriage service reading from the Church of England's updated prayer book.

Arts Page

The Magic Circle has 1,600 members — but has never allowed a woman to join in its 75-year history.

President Mr. Francis White, 74, said: "We like women — they are very good for helping or being cut in half in the box."

The Sun

"HOW ENCHANTED I was by the lovely French actress Cecile Paoli . . . well done the gentleman who cast her in this role!"

Letter in Radio Times.

ALL plurals which do not refer to rational beings are grammatically feminine singular."

Modern Literary Arabic, by David Cohen.

Colin Davis points out, 'Jon has a very considerable technique or he wouldn't be able to do it. He's a man of remarkable discipline and also of exceptional physical strength. Several leading ladies have proudly shown their bruises after singing with Vickers.'

Gillian Widdicombe profiling the tenor Jon Vickers, Observer.

★ ★ ★

"MY AMBITION is to have a show in London with the same sort of reputation that the Crazy Gang had. It would be glamorous, spicy, but above all a family show. People would bring their wives, mothers, and children."

Kenn Dodd in Woman magazine.

Origins uncovers the riddle of the Sphinx, and finds him sadly in need of restoration. 4.2 pm

YOGA FOR MEN

John Champ

This highly original book is guaranteed to generate male interest in yoga. The informative text is complimented by beautiful full page colour photographs of well known models illustrating the postures described. The result is a book that is a joy to look at as well as an ideal manual for beginners.

IT'S THE MEAT IN THE SANDWICH THAT COUNTS!

Rank Theatres House Magazine

It's got all the ingredients for a good love story. Beth, the heroine, has to forsake her nursing career to look after a motherless family. Then there are two young doctors entangled in her life and Beth has much to endure before she finds happiness with the man of her choice.

Woman's reading, I think, light and absorbing.

Ipswich Mercury.

Flannery O'Connor's collection of short stories Everything That Rises Must Converge *was reprinted on September 22 by Faber, £2.95, as were his novels* Wise Blood *and* The Violent Bear It Away.

The Guardian.

★ ★ ★

Motoring

Ad in the Surrey-Hants Star.

Cannock magistrates grinned when told driver Richard Proster had sent his wife's driving licence to be endorsed on a speeding charge.
"I don't blame him at all!" said Mr. Harold Pritchard, sitting in the chair.

Wolverhampton Express and Star, April 25.

"ALTHOUGH this was my first marriage, it was far from being my first Volvo. I always keep them for two years and then trade them in for a new one. I was beginning to think as we drove along in silence that this trade-in policy on cars would soon be followed by a similar one on wives."

Ad. in the Financial Times.

Fortunately, Mrs Hargrave is still, as she so ably demonstrated, a road hazard, switching on windscreen wipers every time she attempts a right-hand turn. But then don't all women drivers?

Martin Jackson, Daily Mail.

"THE GIRLS put pressure on their boyfriends because they want to go out with them. And they like too the idea of it being recognised that they have a man in command."

Spokesmen for Devon County Road Safety Unit quoted in L-rider story in the Daily Mail.

She's a bit like the barmaid at the local. Not exactly pretty. Not unattractive either. But she's got that sort of odd 'something'. The 'something' that would make you want to take her off to the woods, and sort of, see what she's like. If you know what I mean.

Description of a motorcycle in Hondaway magazine.

WHY is it that women are such bad drivers? . . . If you see a car travelling at twenty miles per hour along the middle of a main road so that no one can overtake, you can be sure the driver is a woman!"

Royal Society of Arts Examinations Boards, passage for Aural comprehension.

Join the Professionals

The Union of Drivers for Drivers invite you to come and join them - don't delay

A Japanese car manufacturer has invented the world's first computerized backseat driver which scolds motorists in querulous high-pitched female tones if they forget some driving rules.

If a driver tries to leave his car with his keys in the ignition the voice will declare in petulant female tones: "Make sure you have your keys."

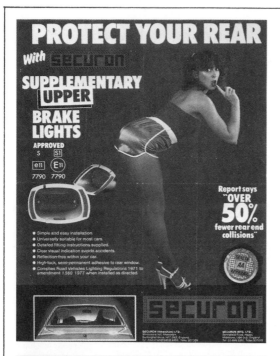

The Inner Ape

PRETTY car girl Margarent Mellor won a battle yesterday against the nightclub bosses who sacked her when she was expecting a baby.

An unrepentant Mr Growns said: "We sell booze and sex in the nicest way and it is offensive for customers to be confronted with a pregnant woman."

The Sun.

A champagne cork should leave the bottle with a sigh like the sound of a contented woman.

Exit Wine Bars wine list.

Susan won, but I do agree with the licensee. Prints are man size. Pints are for guzzling. Pints are masculine.

Let us have our ladies sweet and gentle when they cheer our pubs and clubs.

A Babycham for the lady, please.

With a cherry.

John Field ("The column with the Sunday punch"), News of the World.

GOOD FOOD is like a mistress — expensive but worth it. Bad food is like a wife — trouble all day long.

Menu, Earl of Doncaster Hotel, Doncaster.

Councillor Charlotte Toal questioned the need to employ a tea-taster and offered to do the job herself.

Mr McCulloch said: "It's not as easy as the lady thinks. I have been in the business since 1946 and taste about 1000 samples a week.

"Teas can be like some women — all dressed up and looking fine but basically no good."

Glasgow Herald.

RESTAURANT owner Jerry Hermann found business boomed when he decided to make his pizzas in the shape of a woman's bust.

Now sales have trebled at his restaurant in Evanston, Illinois.

"People can buy them in three bra sizes—A, B or C," says Jerry. "Most of my customers are middle-aged men."

News of the World.

If you're at your wits' end to know what to do with the family, perhaps packing them off on a four-day basic cookery course would be the answer. The fee is £85, which you might think a high price to teach a girl to cook - but would it not be worth it for a boy?

The Observer

Ape at Large

THERE is not such a large demand for animal studies . . However, those that are used fall into two categories: for male designs: Alsatians (sic), Great Danes, Boxers, etc., and for female designs: Poodles, puppies and almost any fluffy appealing cat or dog.

Wilson Bros. Greeting Cards Ltd., in newsletter of the Bureau of Freelance Photographers.

HOW CAN a housewife be expected to answer obscure questions about Chekhov . . .?

Oxford Star preview of Mastermind.

The couple are thought to be in their twenties. Mr. Finlay said: "They may well be a normal married couple or it may be a case of a man with another man's wife, or vice versa.

The Guardian.

" LAUNDRY WORKER Sheila Denyer (38), from Okehampton in Devon chooses The Bible as her specialised subject in the fifth heat of Mastermind to be screened on Sunday, September 18. Surprisingly she is joined by another female, Penzance housewife Josephine Lawrey (50) . . ."

BBC Television publicity handout.

"YOU SEE, just like any other woman, give her a good hair-do and she bucks up straight away."

Peter Woods on Ching-Ching, BBC news.

"HOME SLIDE shows are often far more interesting than the television programmes. And sooner or later, the women of the house will brighten each member of the assembly by asking: 'Would you like a cup of tea?' "

The Dalesman.

"I AGREE with W. C. Fields who said that women are like elephants - nice to look at but who wants to own one?"

Warren Beatty, quoted in Girl About Town.

Formless it certainly was. The BBC commentator was a woman. Perhaps she had been landed with the shift because it was the holiday and the men were out relaxing, who knows? Or perhaps the Bank Holiday shift is coveted and, in a new age, Equalised Woman gets the plum. Perhaps the men wanted to watch John Wayne. Either way through no fault of her own the poor lady was lost, and so at first were we.

John Le Carré on the Prince's Gate siege, Observer

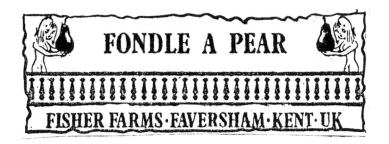

FISHER FARMS·FAVERSHAM·KENT·UK

SHEARING SHEEP

Rathmell Young Farmers' Club met at Rome Farm, Giggleswick when sheep shearing and fleece wrapping competitions were held for the boys, while the girls made daisy chains.

Craven News

★ ★ ★

Dorrington Young Farmers Club held a split meeting at Longnor Village Hall when the boys were given a talk by a gunsmith and the girls had a talk on poultry trussing.

Shropshire Star.

Sir. — It seems naive of the Playboy Club to believe they could sack a bunny girl for being pregnant (Guardian October 10).
After all, as any schoolboy could tell them, popular opinion would be that the girl had only behaved like any other rabbit. — Yours

Letter to the Guardian.

★ ★ ★

But the awards will not just go to the famous.
A warm-hearted traffic warden . . . a brave schoolboy . . . a beautiful girl . . . anyone who is worth mentioning in the Daily Star

Daily Star, Gold Award scheme.

"REGULARS celebrated by trying to sell off the barmaid. But she was finally withdrawn from the auction because regulars couldn't decide who should buy her. Another surprise was the auctioning of three tons of manure."

Western Daily Press And Times And Mirror.

"The goose was fine with me. I keep them at home in Sussex and know how to treat them. It's rather like looking after a wife or a dog. You tuck them under your arm, stroke their necks and whistle to them.

Daily Mail.

"WIVES are like dogs—they resent coming to heel but they need to be exercised regularly."

Lucy Ashton, Sunday Express.

Birthdays

● Today—Dame Ruth Railton (Mrs Cecil King), founder and former musical director of National Youth Orchestra.

Sunday Times.

At 55 Whicker, born in Cairo to an Army officer father, is a rare thing: in

The Times

Now The Times is going to fight for herself

by William Rees-Mogg

Quicker by rail?

From Mrs. J.K. Emery

Sir, The High Speed Train from London to Bristol takes only an hour and a half. Fine. Last week I went to catch it and queued for 25 minutes at Paddington's ticket office. Perhaps we need some High Speed Stations.

Yours faithfully,
JOAN BAKEWELL
20 Chalcot Square, NW1.

The Times

★ ★ ★

On the plane home from Los Angeles last week I turned on the Plain Girl Power. I'm not exactly *plain,* but I do use the "power". This is how it works: You listen to the man 90 per cent of the time, talk *ten* and he thinks you're the most devastating conversationalist he ever heard! I learned this technique from my favourite magazine. It works with people other than men, of course, though I've seen my airplane friend twelve times since we met. Blessings on the power and the magazine! I guess you could say I'm That COSMO-POLITAN Girl.

Ad. for Cosmopolitan in the American magazine Advertising Age

IN THE Mediterranean as elsewhere, everybody has a father and a mother, most have siblings, most have wives and children.

People of the Mediterranean, by J. Davies

the basic facts are indisputable. Frank Thomas Robertson Giles was born 61 years and seven months ago, the only son of Colonel F. L. N. Giles, DSO, OBE, and wife.

Atticus's profile of his new editor in the Sunday Times.

★ ★ ★

"YOUR INTERESTS may be fairly ordinary; you like to read a little, go to the cinema, theatre, an occasional concert . . . Or you may, if you are a woman, enjoy spending a lot of time window shopping."

Lesson XI of The Journalism Course, published by the London School of Journalism Ltd.

★ ★ ★

LAST YEAR was a very good year for Buckinghamshire in terms of man-made production levels at least. For the latest figures available reveal the county enjoyed a baby boom

Bucks Examiner.

★ ★ ★

MR HERBERT SMITH is the only man among the 54 members of St Mark's Evergreen Club, Leicester . . . so they elected him the club leader.

Leicester Mercury.

"THE cost of each shower should not exceed 3p. This is, without question, the most inexpensive method of keeping your wife and children clean."

Popular DIY magazine.

collars were inelegant garments. A well-starched collar adds a unique final touch to a gentleman's suit. Cost apart, the problem is how to get a collar *properly* starched. In these days when home industries are starting up for every,hing, wives might find recapturing the art of starching an amusing diversion. Also a method of control, a

Some of the unemployed drivers say that they have worked for the Guernsey Railway Co. for up to 30 years. With such long service to their credit they say they cannot understand why staff who have been with the old company for only a year or two have been given work.
'They have even employed a woman driver!' said one former driver with a long record of service.

Annual trip — Four coaches transported aged members, wives, widows, and friends of the Workingmen's Club, Wheatley Hill, to South Shields, for their annual day out. Lunch was provided, and £3 was given to each man, and £1 to each woman.

Hartlepool Mail.

The two highlights in her life, however, were her husband's outstandingly successful terms of office as Governor-General of South Africa from 1924-30 and of Canada from 1940-45.

What went wrong ? Friends say that because of the long separations it was always an "anguished romance." Now Marcelle, like most bachelor girls over 30, is looking for a "good man" with marriage possibilities.

WHY IS A SHIP CALLED SHE ?

A ship is called a 'she' because there is always a great deal of bustle around her; there is usually a gang of men about, she has a waist and stays; it takes a lot of paint to keep her good looking; it is not the initial expense that breaks you, it is the upkeep; she can be all decked out; it takes an experienced man to handle her correctly; and without a man at the helm, she is absolutely uncontrollable. She shows her topsides, hides her bottom and, when coming into port, always heads for the buoys.

From an Irish Linen tea cloth.

Mrs Housewife This cistern is fitted with our patented

QUIET BALLVALVE

Armitage Shanks sticker.

NAVAL & MILITARY CLUB,

94, PICCADILLY,

LONDON, W1V OBP

(LADIES' ENTRANCE - 42 HALF MOON STREET)

"IT'S ON hot days like today when you see everyone in summer dresses that the female species doesn't seem such a blatant design fault after all."

Nail Taylor, Kent News Shopper.

★ ★ ★

"THIS questionnaire should be filled in by the housewife as most of the questions deal with washing and clothing."

Consumer test form

WHY worry about equal rights? All a woman has to do to get a man's salary is to marry one.

Hull Star.

Girl shows men the art of stripping

Yorkshire Post Correspondent

A 20-YEAR-OLD wife, who enjoyed stripping down under the watchful gaze of a dozen men, has every reason to be proud of her bodywork.

Mrs. Debbie Lindley was the only girl among 12 men who took a Government training scheme to learn how to strip down and respray cars. Now she is starting work with a temporary job at a garage at Doncaster.

Yorkshire Post.

"WHERE the lessee is a female, or a company or other artificial person 'or consists of two or more persons this lease shall be construed with the appropriate amendments . . ."

Extract from a lease.

"I CAN never make up my mind . . . typical woman."

Helen Liddell, secretary of the Labour Party in Scotland, Any Questions, Radio 4.

"WHO invented gunpowder?"
"A woman who wanted guns to look pretty."

Penguin joke book.

DON'T MAKE A BOOB
COME TO
TRADE CARPETS WAREHOUSE

Hampstead and Highgate Express

HOW TO TREAT THE WIFE!

GIVE HER AS MUCH MONEY AS SHE WANTS FOR CLOTHES, ONE ARMED BANDITS AND BINGO!

DO ALL THE HOUSEWORK WHILE SHE WATCHES TELEVISION!

NEVER GO OUT BOOZING WITH THE BOYS—NEVER SMOKE!

TELL HER YOU LOVE HER EVERY DAY.

LET HER HAVE ANYTHING SHE WANTS

AND IF THAT DOESN'T SATISFY HER —

DROWN THE SILLY OLD MOO!

WE WOMEN MUST NOT TAKE THINGS LYING DOWN—WE WILL NOT BE JUMPED ON—WE MUST STICK THINGS OUT TOGETHER—AS LONG AS WE ARE SPLIT—THOSE MALE CHAUVINIST PIGS WILL BE ON TOP OF US!

WOMENS LIB RALLY!

WOMENS LI

SHE'LL BE LUCKY MAVIS!

"Some women want their breasts improved because they feel their husbands have gone off them. The truth may be that they have let themselves go, and what they should do is get a new dress, have a hair-do and cook him a good meal for when he gets home."

Daily Telegraph.

AMOROSA, n. a wanton woman.
AMOROSO, n. a lover: a man enamoured.

Nuttall's Standard Dictionary of the English Language, Fifth Edition, reprinted 1936.

26 Across — Clue: Seducing a bird could be productive (6,3). Answer: Laying Hen.
19 Across — Clue: What Dad does on the quiet? (5,3). Answer: Keeps Mum.

Guardian Crossword 15,752.

"IF you want your wife to act more like a mistress start treating her like one. Buy her diamonds this Christmas!"

Ad in the Stevenage Midweek Gazette.

AU CHAPITRE DE LA NOUVEAUTÉ

Il existe des chaussures de femmes dont les hautes semelles et les hauts talons sont amovibles. Selon les circonstances – et la taille de l'homme avec lequel elle sort – la femme peut à volonté les fixer ou les enlever.

Le Bien Public (Bourgogne's daily paper).

Why not give a bathmat on Mother's Day

Eastern Evening News

FOR DADS
360
bottles of whisky

FOR MUMS
100
Turkeys

Man's love for a bit of high risk adventure will be demonstrated at the weekend by two Conisbrough girls who, along with their boyfriends have agreed to try out all the daredevil stomach-churning rides in Blackpool.

"THE needles of sewing and stitching machines were responsible for 31 accidents . . . Considering the large number of women and girls who work in the closing rooms, this number was not large."

Choice of Careers booklet on the footwear industry.

"ONCE YOU calculate the cost of a housekeeper and someone to care for your children, you'll find that adequate protection for your wife is a necessity, not a luxury."

AA insurance brochure.

"I HAVE a huge collection of books which are enjoyed by all my family, expect my wife, whose job it is to dust them."

Harry Secombe in book handout to junior schools.

"It will have Everything Women Want," raves producer Jerry Spangler. "Men, money, jewellery, castles, caviar, champagne and love, love, love."

Sunday Times.

And Mr Redford should be warned. The thinking woman of the Western World is not ready for two hunks of intellectual beefcake on the same programme.
She needs the sexy old crooked smile, and a glimpse of Hollywood muscle to feed her fantasy, too.

Daily Express.

Last month the 39-year-old meat baron announced that after several domestic upheavals their 10-year marriage was finally over. Part of the problems has been Kate's in ability to provide an heir — they have two daughters.

New Standard report of Lord Vestey's divorce

"CHILDREN have seen flying saucers; housewives have seen them, and even dogs. Perhaps we do not think that the opinions of children, housewives - or dogs are important. But schoolteachers have also seen them, and Air Force officers, judges and even policemen."

Reading for Adults by
J. R. Lewis (Longman, 1971)

"EVEN someone middle aged, like myself, does not find it much fun when travelling having to look after one's wife and one's luggage."

Lord Mowbray and Stourton,
House of Lords.

"HOW SOON after you were dropped in Yugoslavia were you able to discover that Tito was in fact a real person and not, as some people thought, a woman?"

Sue MacGregor talking to
Sir Fitzroy Maclean, Radio 4.

"BEAUTY, complexion, personality, talent and, yes, even brains were discussed as the 66 competitors paraded their obvious charms. But how good are they at washing the dishes, cooking, or housework? Surely these are the more important female requirements."

Sporting Life reporting the
Miss World contest.

GET 'EM DOWN SAFELY WITH AIR TRAFFIC CONTROL

Women are much more unstable. They burst into tears at the drop of a hat, they have collywobbles, they go sick for no jolly good reason. My deputy, who is a woman; tends to deal more with their emotional problems. All I can do is smile at them in the corridors, or give them a pat on the head. Does it upset me? Good Lord, no! I'm a married man, so I'm used to women bursting into tears. And I think the prisoners all like having a man around.

John Yates, Governor of
Cookham Wood Women's
Prison, interviewed in
Woman's World.

Another beauty with qualms about the competition last night was Miss Canada. 19-year-old Annette Labrécque, who was on the verge of pulling out.

"I thought this was a personality contest," said Annette. vital statistics 34-23-34.

The Sun.

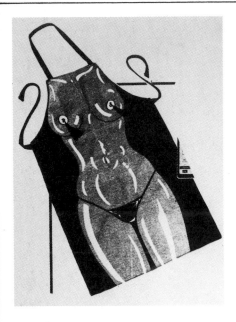

The one militant, from the *Morning Star* (like the writer quoted above) could be no more specific than to complain about women being regarded as 'sex objects'.

If not women, who are men meant to regard as sex objects — horses?

Dog watches Dog. UK Press Gazette.

★ ★ ★

"THE GIRLS, who work on the Aycliffe industrial estate, were chosen for their outstanding features to illustrate the brochure. Mandy Pick was chosen for her shapely body which will be seen oiled. Pauline Chan's pert behind will illustrate the section on recreation.

Sunday Sun.

★ ★ ★

"MOTIVATION . . . is a major factor in the speed and success of learning a foreign language . . . the best asset is a girlfriend from the area you are setting out to explore (a form of back-up often known as 'horizontal Berlitz')."

Executive Travel and Leisure magazine.

★ ★ ★

"BUILDERS have no particular bias against women architects since they regard all architects as women anyway."

Building Magazine.

He pointed out that it was well-known that an Irishman would climb over ten naked women to get to a pint of Guiness, but added that this was possibly the action of an intelligent man.

Shareholder at Guinness annual meeting — Irish Times.

Virginity test husband to press for damages

News Line.

The blonde, whose flight was partly sponsored by the Daily Express, admits that underneath the canvas, furlined jump-suit she is wearing, there is an air of frivolity.

"I'm wearing a pair of frilly black pants and bra," she says.